Grade 5, Book 5

TECHNOLOGY TO THE RESCUE

Contents

Introduction. 2
History 4
Spreader-Cutters. 6
Helicopters. 8
Night-Vision Equipment 10
Thermal-Imaging Equipment. 12
Sonar. 14
The Global Positioning System 16
Robots. 18
Conclusion. 20
Glossary and Index 21
Activities 22

CB123101

INTRODUCTION

Search and rescue (SAR) services help people out of all sorts of dangerous situations. Sometimes, people get lost while hiking or fishing. Sometimes, they are trapped by car crashes, shipwrecks and other accidents. Natural disasters such as earthquakes, floods and cyclones can cause serious destruction and injuries. SAR services can help people in these situations.

SAR work has been happening for centuries. However, teams trained specifically for search and rescue have been around only since the early twentieth century. These teams are sent out to do specific tasks, or **missions**. They use cutting-edge technology.

SAR workers have a very tough job. In trying to save other people, they often put themselves in danger. Any tools that can make their job less dangerous are welcome. This is where modern technology can help. Technology can also help people who may not have otherwise been rescued. In this book, you will learn about some of the technology rescue workers use.

Flash floods can cause deaths and injuries.

High winds can destroy property and endanger lives.

Earthquakes can destroy buildings and trap people under rubble.

HISTORY

Throughout history, people have needed rescuing. Even before there were organised SAR teams, technology was used to try to help people in need of rescue.

One of the earliest documented SAR operations took place in the seventeenth century. A Dutch merchant ship, the *Vergulde Draeck*, struck a reef and sank off the coast of Western Australia in 1656. Seventy-five survivors made it to shore. Australia was very remote in those days, so seven men used a small boat to go to Batavia, modern-day Jakarta in Indonesia, for help.

Two ships were immediately sent on an SAR mission. Sadly, they failed to find the survivors. A year later, a second mission with one ship was sent. It, too, failed. A further six months later, two more ships were sent. This third and final mission also failed.

Three different types of ships were used in the searches – galliots, flutes and a yacht. They carried the best technology available at the time for directing the course of a ship, called **navigating equipment**. This would have included a maritime compass. However, the survivors were never rescued. We cannot know if modern navigating equipment would have made a difference.

Over the last 100 years, many groups have been set up specifically to search for and rescue people. SAR workers get special training. They use all kinds of equipment. They use some simple equipment, such as binoculars. They also use complex technology, such as equipment that detects heat, or **thermal-imaging equipment**.

A full-scale copy of a seventeenth-century ship that was very similar to the *Vergulde Draeck*

THE ROUTE SHIPS TOOK FROM AMSTERDAM TO BATAVIA

SPREADER-CUTTERS

Often called 'the jaws of life', spreader-cutters are one of the most important pieces of rescue equipment available. SAR workers use spreader-cutters to release people trapped in collapsed buildings or cars.

Spreader-cutters are a very simple piece of technology, but they are very effective. How are they used? Here is an example. A person is trapped inside a wrecked car. The door is buckled and jammed shut. The tips of the spreader-cutter's blades are wedged into a small gap around the door. A water-powered pump, called a **hydraulic pump**, spreads the blades apart. This forces the gap to widen. The open blades are then positioned around the metal. The pump action is reversed to close the blades. The blades cut through the metal like a giant pair of scissors.

A hydraulic spreader-cutter

Once the gap is wide enough, the person can be removed from the wreckage.

Spreader-cutters can also be used to lift heavy objects. The blades are wedged between the ground and the object. The hydraulic pump opens the spreader-cutter's blades, which lifts up the heavy object. In this way, spreader-cutters are often used to free people from under wreckage.

Spreader-cutters allow SAR workers to open gaps in metal very quickly. They are a lot quicker than using a saw, which would create sparks as it cut through the metal.

Firefighters using a hydraulic spreader-cutter on a wrecked car

HELICOPTERS

The use of helicopters in SAR work was first tested during World War II, which began in 1939. They were better for rescuing downed airmen than planes. They could land in many places because they did not need a runway.

In April 1944, a Sikorsky R-4 helicopter was used in a daring rescue. The helicopter could only carry one airman at a time, but three downed airmen were rescued from the jungle in Burma (Myanmar). After the Vietnam War started in 1959, the Sikorsky HH-3E Jolly Green Giant helicopter became the main SAR helicopter. It, too, was used to rescue downed airmen, but it was much larger and could carry more than one person at a time. The use of helicopters for SAR has since spread to non-military operations, or **civilian operations**.

There are two important things an SAR helicopter needs to be able to do. It needs to be able to fly long distances. It also needs to be able to mount a device used to pull in a heavy load, or a winch. A winch is used to lift the person being rescued to safety. This is important, because sometimes the helicopter cannot land. For example, an injured hiker may need to be lifted out of a forest or the crew of a ship may need to be pulled out of rough water.

A man photographing the rotor blades of a model Sikorsky R-4 helicopter in 1944

Above: A Sikorsky HH-3E Jolly Green Giant taking off in Vietnam in 1968

Left: An SAR team practising helicopter rescues at sea

NIGHT-VISION EQUIPMENT

Night-vision equipment is used to help people see in the dark. There is a huge range of night-vision equipment, from goggles to binoculars to cameras. This equipment can be of great use to SAR teams working at night.

Night-vision equipment was first made for military use. It has since found uses in civilian operations. It is used for all kinds of things. It is used for scientific research, wildlife photography, security work, police work and SAR work.

Night-vision equipment uses the natural light that is present, such as moonlight. It enhances that light and produces a green-tinged image. This type of equipment cannot operate in 100-per-cent darkness. It needs at least a little bit of light. However, even during the night, there is always some light present.

Helicopter pilots can wear special goggles at night. When searching for people at night, rescuers often use night vision binoculars as well. Night-vision equipment has saved many people. Lost hikers have been found. Survivors of boating accidents have been rescued. With night-vision equipment, SAR workers do not have to stop working when it gets dark. They can continue to search. This means there is more chance of finding people alive.

A night-vision image of a man using his own night-vision binoculars

A helicopter seen with the help of night-vision equipment

THERMAL-IMAGING EQUIPMENT

Thermal-imaging equipment allows SAR workers to search large areas quickly and accurately. They can use this equipment during the day or night and in all sorts of weather. They can use it in rain or fog. It is also useful in bright sunlight, when glare makes it hard to see.

A type of light that cannot be seen by human eyes is **infrared light**. Almost all objects give off infrared light. The hotter an object, the more infrared light it gives off. It is possible to measure and record this light.

A thermal camera

Thermal-imaging equipment senses infrared light. It measures the different amounts of light given off by different objects. Then it makes the measurements into an image. Thermal images can be quite colourful. Different colours represent different temperatures. Blue shows the coldest parts and red shows the hottest parts.

Here is an example of how thermal-imaging equipment is used. A ship has sunk. It is raining and the sea is rough. It is hard to see anything. SAR workers in a helicopter can use thermal-imaging equipment. They look on their screen for red dots, showing the body temperature of a person, against the blue background of the cold sea.

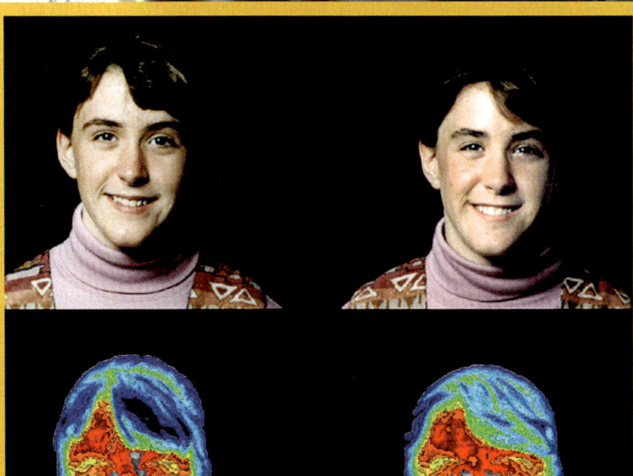

Above: Firefighters in the United States use thermal imaging to investigate the cause of a fire

Left: Photographs (above) and thermal images (below) of identical twin sisters

SONAR

Some people die before SAR workers can get to them. Searching for bodies is one of the worst jobs that SAR workers do. Sonar can help them carry out this task.

Finding drowning victims is hard. These types of searches often involve divers and underwater cameras. It can be dangerous work. Sometimes, it is hard to see. Strong currents and underwater objects can cause problems. These searches can also take a long time. The search area is often large. Sometimes, witnesses cannot give an exact location. Often, there are no witnesses. Many searches end without finding the bodies.

A man preparing a sonar for use

Sonar devices use sound to detect underwater objects. The kind of sonar used by SAR teams is called **side scan sonar**. A boat tows the sonar device at a speed of about 3.2 kilometres per hour. The sonar device emits fan-shaped pulses of sound. The sound goes down towards the floor of the ocean, lake or river. The floor and any objects on it reflect the sound back to the side scan sonar. The pulses are analysed and turned into computer images. Sonar equipment can search dark, murky water. It can search large areas quickly. SAR workers watch a screen and look for body-shaped images.

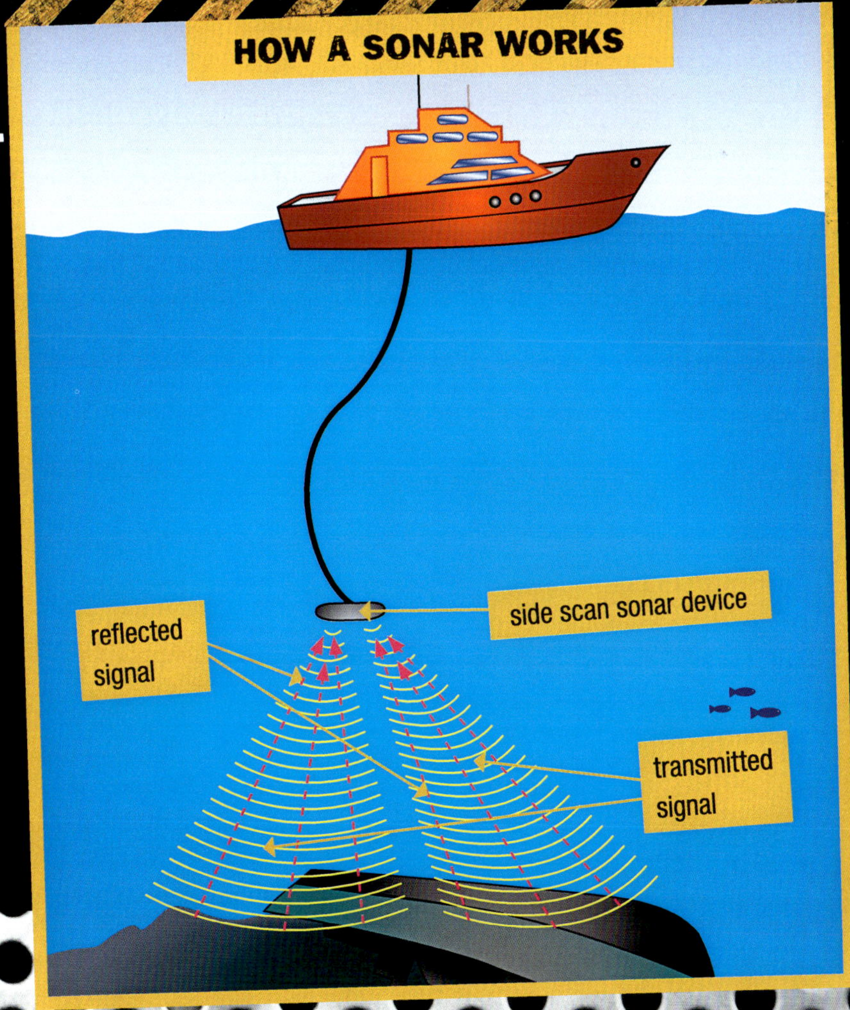

THE GLOBAL POSITIONING SYSTEM

The Global Positioning System (GPS) is a system of orbiting satellites. They provide navigation data to users all over the world. Many cars now have GPS. It allows people to get street directions as they are travelling. This same system is now used for SAR work.

The satellites send out navigation signals. People can receive these signals if they are carrying the right equipment. The signals can show their exact location. They can also calculate the direction and speed at which a vehicle is travelling. The signals are very accurate. A person's position can be worked out to within about 10 metres.

GPS equipment is now carried on commercial aircraft and ships. It can be used to find the exact position of a ship that is in danger. It can also be used to locate a plane that has crashed or made an emergency landing.

SAR teams also use GPS to coordinate their searches. Here is an example. Three teams are searching a large area of jungle. Each team uses GPS to see where the other teams are searching. This way, the teams can be sure that, together, they search the whole area.

Russian SAR workers using GPS as they search for a spacecraft that strayed from its intended path while returning to Earth

ROBOTS

Robots do all sorts of far-fetched things in movies, but people are using robots in real SAR operations all over the world. They are possibly the ultimate SAR technology.

Robots are used to search for people in dangerous places, such as collapsed buildings or mines. One of the first robots used in SAR operations was the Talon robot. It was designed for use with dangerous, or **hazardous**, materials and bomb disposal. It is now used in SAR operations. It has special equipment to check for hazardous gas and radiation. It also has a robotic arm with a gripping claw and video cameras. This robot is sent into dangerous places to look for people. By sending the robot, no more human lives are put at risk. If the robot finds people, rescue teams know exactly where to go to pick them up. They also know the conditions they will be heading into, so they can be prepared. If they know there is a gas leak, for example, they can wear gas masks.

A Talon robot was used in the United States during rescues at the World Trade Center, after the twin towers were attacked on 11 September 2001. Talon robots are now standard equipment for many SAR teams worldwide. Robots help save the lives of victims. They can save the lives of SAR workers, too.

A Talon robot in Iraq

CONCLUSION

There are SAR teams all over the world. The military runs many SAR teams. Governments set up other civilian SAR teams. There are also many volunteer SAR groups. Rescue South Africa (RSA) is one of the most well known SAR groups in South Africa.

There is even an international group that helps the SAR teams in different countries. It is run by the United Nations. It is called the International Search and Rescue Advisory Group, or INSARAG. RSA is a member of INSARAG.

Wherever there are SAR teams, you can be sure that they will be using all the rescue technology they can lay their hands on. All this technology can be expensive, but saving lives is worth the money!

Rescue workers in South Africa help an injured victim after a train accident.

GLOSSARY

civilian operations – non-military operations

hazardous – dangerous

hydraulic pump – a water-powered pump

infrared light – a kind of light that cannot be seen by human eyes

missions – a specific task that a team is sent to do

navigating equipment – equipment for directing the course of a ship or vehicle

side scan sonar – a sonar device towed by a ship

thermal-imaging equipment – equipment that detects heat

INDEX

binoculars 4, 10, 11

body/bodies 14, 15

camera(s) 10, 12, 14, 18

GPS 16, 17

helicopter(s) 8–11, 13, 20

hydraulic spreader-cutter 6, 7

sonar 14, 15

winch 8

Activities

Genre Focus

Explanation

An explanation is a text that explains how or why things occur or work.

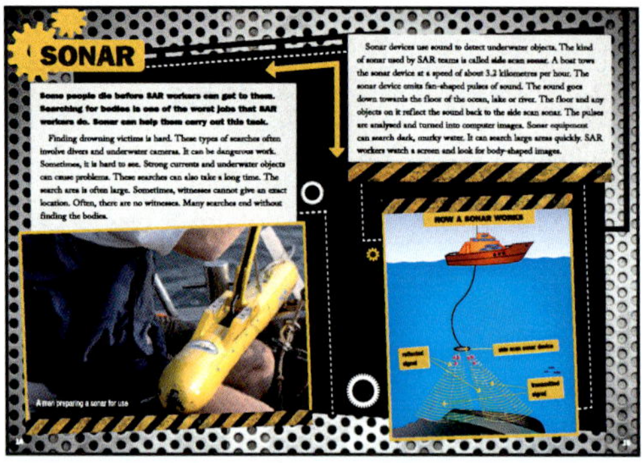

Looking back at an EXPLANATION

Technology to the Rescue is a text that explains how technology is helpful in different rescue situations.

1. This book as a whole is an explanation. But there are a number of mini-explanations within the book. An explanation begins with a statement or statements that tell what is to be explained. Recheck the introduction (page 2), and write a paragraph that tells whether or not you agree with the following statement: 'The first and last sentences of the introduction could be used alone to introduce this text'. Give reasons for your answer.

2. Details of sequential events or stages in operation follow the introduction. There is a mini-explanation about spreader-cutters on pages 6 and 7. The first paragraph introduces the spreader-cutters. Draw a series of ordered pictures that show the details of the operation explained in the next paragraph. Write a supportive sentence under each picture.

3. In three sentences, summarise the conclusion to the whole text (page 20).

4. An explanation has vocabulary that is specific to the topic. List in alphabetical order the topic-specific words that are used in the mini-explanation of thermal imaging (pages 12 and 13).

Writing an Explanation

1. Think for a moment about how often firefighters rescue people from burning buildings. Use a variety of sources to research firefighters and their work. Take notes about the equipment firefighters use, such as trucks, ladders and hoses. You will use your notes to write an explanation text called 'Firefighters to the Rescue'.

2. Write a statement that tells what will be explained. For example: 'Every day, firefighters use their equipment to rescue people in danger'.

3. Now, you need to tell in detail what is done and how it is done. Use your notes to explain what happens once an engine pulls up at a fire – how hoses are unwound and connected to water sources, how ladders are raised and how firefighters reach the victims of fires.

4. Write a concluding statement that rounds off the explanation of the rescues. Check that you have used the present tense and words and phrases that show the order in which things happen. Draw a labelled diagram to support your explanation.

Comprehension Focus

Compare and Contrast

Remember

Compare and contrast is looking at the similarities (comparisons) and differences (contrasts) between aspects of a text, such as characters, events and settings.

1. Draw up a Venn diagram, and write the information below (from pages 8 and 9) in the circles to show the similarities and differences.

   - Sikorsky R-4
   - used in 1959
   - Sikorsky HH-3E
   - used in 1944
   - could rescue more than one person at once
   - could rescue only one person at once
   - used for rescues during war

2. Rule up two columns like those shown below. Copy all the information from Column A into your first column. In Column B, write the correct endings for the sentences in the correct spaces. Use the information in the book to help you.

COLUMN A	COLUMN B
· Both robots and spreader-cutters	can both help in night rescues.
· night-vision and thermal-imaging equipment	with the use of sonar, thermal imaging, or night-vision equipment.
· Rescues at sea can take place	and navigation systems are used on ships today.
· Technology in the form of navigation systems was used on ships back in the seventeenth century	can be used to rescue people trapped in collapsed buildings.